INTERNATIONAL POCKET LIBRARY

EDITED BY EDMUND R. BROWN

THE HOUND OF HEAVEN

AND OTHER POEMS

Francis Thompson
AT THE AGE OF NINETEEN

THE HOUND OF HEAVEN
and Other Poems

FRANCIS THOMPSON

With an Introduction
By G. K. CHESTERTON

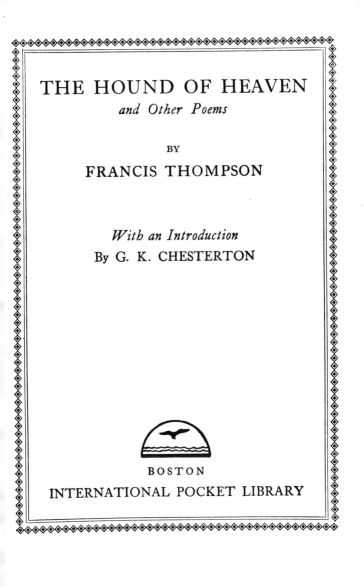

BOSTON
INTERNATIONAL POCKET LIBRARY

B｜B

BRANDEN BOOKS
P.O. Box 812094
Wellesley MA 02482

INTRODUCTION

BY G. K. CHESTERTON

'THE HOUND OF HEAVEN,' the greatest religious poem of modern times and one of the greatest of all times, was produced under certain peculiar historical conditions, which accentuate its isolation. To begin with, the religious poem is a religious poem, not only in what we should call the real sense, but in what some would call the limited sense. The word 'religion' is used in these days in an expansive or telescopic fashion, sometimes inevitable, sometimes nearly intolerable. It is used of various realms of emotion or spiritual speculation more or less lying on the borders of religion itself; it is applied to other things that have nothing to do with religion; it is applied to some things that are almost identical with irreligion. But the line between legitimate and illegitimate expansion of a word is so difficult to draw, that there is little to be gained by questioning it, except that mere quarrel about a word that is called logomachy. There always are some confusions about a definition or exceptions to a rule. The great principle that Pigs Is Pigs does not dispose entirely of the existence of pig-iron, or of cannibals calling a man a long pig. We all know the plain practical man, the sceptic in the crowd, the atheist on the soap-box, who boasts that he calls a spade a spade, and generally calls it a spyde. But even he may have to deal with the learned and sophisticated man, who will prove to him that, even in the case of the ace of spades which he planks down in playing poker, the spade is not really a spade; being derived from the Spanish *espada*, a sword. If once we begin to quibble and quarrel about what words ought to mean, or can be made to mean, we shall find ourselves in a mere world of words, most wearisome to those who are concerned with thoughts. For the latter it will be enough to realise that there certainly was and is a certain *thing,* to which our fathers found it more practical to attach and limit the name of religion; that they recognised that the thing had many forms, and that there were many religions; but that they were equally certain of what things were not religions, including much that modern moralists call a wider religious life. They recognised a Protestant religion and a Catholic religion, and probably thought one or other of them true; they recognised a Mohammedan religion, even if they thought it false; they recognised a Jewish religion, which had once been true and by a sort of treason had become false; and so on. But they did not recognise a Religion of Humanity; or a 'Religion of the Life Force'; or a religion of creative evolution; or a religion which has the object of ultimately producing a god who does not yet exist. And the distinction is better preserved by noting these examples than by an attempt to fix the elusive evasions of the verbal sophists of today.

What we mean, when we say that 'The Hound of Heaven' is a real religious poem, is simply that it would make no sense, if we supposed it to refer to any of these modern abstractions, or to anything but a personal Creator in relation to a personal creature. It may be and indeed is a generous and charitable mood to look out on all the multitudes of men with sympathy and social loyalty. But it was not the multitudes of men that were pursuing the hero of this poem 'down the nights and down the days.' It may be a good thing for men to look forward to mankind some day producing a superior being, thousands of years hence, who will be like a god compared with the common mass of

[6]

men. But it was not some superior person born a thousand years hence, who drove the sinner in this story from refuge to refuge. He was not running away from the Life Force; from a mere summary of all natural vitality; which would be expressed equally in the pursued or the pursuer. For it requires quite as much Life Force to run away from anybody as to run after anybody. He was not swiftly escaping from a slow adaptive process called evolution, like a man pursued by a snail. He was not alarmed at a gradual biological transformation, by which a Hound of Heaven might be evolved out of a Hound of Hell. He was dealing with the direct individual relations of God and Man, and the story would be absolutely senseless to anybody who thought that the service of Man is a substitute for the service of God. This is where the practical habit of speech, among our religious ancestors of all religions, proves its validity and veracity. Francis Thompson was a Catholic, and a very Catholic Catholic. In some aspects of art, poetry and pomp the Catholic is more akin to the Pagan; in some aspects of philosophy and logic (though this is little understood) he has more sympathy with the sceptic or the agnostic. But in the solid central fact of the subject or subject-matter, he is still something utterly separate from sceptics and even from pagans; and all Christians have their part in him. A perfectly simple and straightforward member of the Salvation Army knows what 'The Hound of Heaven' is about, even if he knows it better without reading it; and would recognise its central theology as promptly as the Pope. But the mere Humanist, the mere Humanitarian, the universal aesthete, the patroniser of all religions, he will never know what it was about; for he has never been near enough to God to run away from Him.

[7]

Now the next point of interest is that this poem of purely personal religion, so directly devotional, so dogmatically orthodox, appeared at a time when it might least be expected, and at the end of an historical process that might have seemed to make it impossible. The nineteenth century had been, at least on the surface, one triumphal procession of progress, away from these theological relations, which were accounted narrow, towards ideals of brotherhood or natural living which seemed to be more and more broad. We might say that the poets had led the procession; for even at the beginning of the nineteenth century Shelley and Landor and Byron and Keats had moved in various ways towards a pantheistic paganism; and the tendency was continued by Victor Hugo in Europe and by Walt Whitman in America. There were, of course, continual cross-currents and confusions. Even an appeal to pantheism is something like an appeal to theism, and it was difficult to imitate the pagans without discovering, like St. Paul, that they were very religious. The contradiction came out quaintly in the case of Swinburne, who was always trying to prove that he was an atheist by invoking about ten different gods in a style exactly copied from the Old Testament.

Roughly speaking, however, I myself remember fairly well the curious cultural conditions in which the genius of Francis Thompson arose; for, though I was a boy at the time, a boy can sometimes absorb the atmosphere of a society, with the same subtle subconscious instinct with which a child can absorb the atmosphere of a house. I read all the minor poets; and it was especially an age of minor poets. The curious thing is that Francis Thompson was considered, criticised, appreciated or admired, as one of the minor poets. I can remember Mr. Richard Le Gal-

[8]

lienne, who is one of the survivors of that epoch, defending himself with spirit, but with a certain air of audacity, against the charge of fulsome exaggeration in saying that there was in the poems of this Mr. Thompson an Elizabethan richness and sometimes almost a Shakespearean splendour. Mr. Le Gallienne was quite right; but the main point is that his defence was a general defence of minor poets, and of this poet as a minor poet. It had hardly occurred to the world in general that Francis Thompson was a major poet; we might almost say a major prophet. There was in all that world of culture an atmosphere of paganism that had worn rather thin. But hardly anybody thought that the future of poetry could be anything but a future of paganism. It was then, in the slowly deepening silence as in the poem of Coventry Patmore, that there was first heard, afar off, the baying of a hound.

That is the primary point about the work of Francis Thompson; even before its many-coloured pageant of images and words. The awakening of the *Domini canes*, the Dogs of God, meant that the hunt was up once more; the hunt for the souls of men; and that religion of that *realistic* sort was anything but dead. In Patmore's poem the dog is 'an old guard-hound'; and we may say, without irreverence that the first impression or lesson was that there is life in the old dog yet. In any case, it was an event of history, as much as an event of literature, when personal religion returned suddenly with something of the power of Dante or the *Dies Irae*, after a century in which such religion had seemed to grow more weak and provincial, and more and more impersonal religions appeared to possess the future. And those who best understand the world know that the world is changed; and that the hunt will continue until the world turns to bay.

CONTENTS

THE HOUND OF HEAVEN

I fled Him, down the nights and down the days;
  I fled Him, down the arches of the years;
I fled Him, down the labyrinthine ways
  Of my own mind; and in the mist of tears
I hid from Him, and under running laughter.
      Up vistaed hopes I sped;
      And shot, precipitated,
Adown Titanic glooms of chasmèd fears,
  From those strong Feet that followed, followed after.
      But with unhurrying chase,
      And unperturbèd pace,
  Deliberate speed, majestic instancy,
      They beat—and a Voice beat
      More instant than the Feet—
'All things betray thee, who betrayest Me.'

      I pleaded, outlaw-wise,
By many a hearted casement, curtained red,
  Trellised with intertwining charities;
(For, though I knew His love Who followèd,
      Yet was I sore adread
Lest, having Him, I must have naught beside.)
But, if one little casement parted wide,
  The gust of His approach would clash it to:
  Fear wist not to evade, as Love wist to pursue.
Across the margent of the world I fled,
  And troubled the gold gateways of the stars,
  Smiting for shelter on their clangèd bars;
      Fretted to dulcet jars
And silvern chatter the pale ports o' the moon.

I said to Dawn: Be sudden—to Eve: Be soon;
  With thy young skiey blossoms heap me over
    From this tremendous Lover—
Float thy vague veil about me, lest He see!
  I tempted all His servitors, but to find
My own betrayal in their constancy,
In faith to Him their fickleness to me,
  Their traitorous trueness, and their loyal deceit.
To all swift things for swiftness did I sue;
  Clung to the whistling mane of every wind.
      But whether they swept, smoothly fleet,
    The long savannahs of the blue;
      Or whether, Thunder-driven,
    They clanged his chariot 'thwart a heaven,
Plashy with flying lightnings round the spurn o' their feet:—
  Fear wist not to evade as Love wist to pursue.
      Still with unhurrying chase,
      And unperturbèd pace,
    Deliberate speed, majestic instancy,
      Came on the following Feet,
      And a Voice above their beat—
  'Naught shelters thee, who wilt not shelter Me.'

I sought no more that after which I strayed
        In face of man or maid;
But still within the little children's eyes
      Seems something, something that replies,
They at least are for me, surely for me!
I turned me to them very wistfully;
But just as their young eyes grew sudden fair
      With dawning answers there,
Their angel plucked them from me by the hair.

[12]

'Come then, ye other children, Nature's—share
With me' (said I) 'your delicate fellowship;
      Let me greet you lip to lip,
      Let me twine with you caresses,
         Wantoning
      With our Lady-Mother's vagrant tresses,
         Banqueting
      With her in her wind-walled palace,
      Underneath her azured daïs,
      Quaffing, as your taintless way is,
         From a chalice
Lucent-weeping out of the dayspring.'
      So it was done:
I in their delicate fellowship was one—
Drew the bolt of Nature's secrecies.
      I knew all the swift importings
      On the wilful face of skies;
      I knew how the clouds arise
      Spumèd of the wild sea-snortings;
         All that's born or dies
      Rose and drooped with; made them shapers
Of mine own moods, or wailful divine;
      With them joyed and was bereaven.
      I was heavy with the even,
      When she lit her glimmering tapers
      Round the day's dead sanctities.
      I laughed in the morning's eyes.
I triumphed and I saddened with all weather,
      Heaven and I wept together,
And its sweet tears were salt with mortal mine:
Against the red throb of its sunset-heart
      I laid my own to beat,
      And share commingling heat;

But not by that, by that, was eased my human smart.
In vain my tears were wet on Heaven's grey cheek.
For ah! we know not what each other says,
      These things and I; in sound *I* speak—
Their sound is but their stir, they speak by silences.
Nature, poor stepdame, cannot slake my drouth;
      Let her, if she would owe me,
Drop yon blue bosom-veil of sky, and show me
      The breasts o' her tenderness:
Never did any milk of hers once bless
      My thirsting mouth.
      Nigh and nigh draws the chase,
      With unperturbèd pace,
  Deliberate speed, majestic instancy;
      And past those noisèd Feet
      A voice comes yet more fleet—
'Lo! naught contents thee, who content'st not Me.'

Naked I wait Thy love's uplifted stroke!
My harness piece by piece Thou hast hewn from me,
      And smitten me to my knee;
      I am defenceless utterly.
      I slept, methinks, and woke,
And, slowly gazing, find me stripped in sleep.
In the rash lustihead of my young powers,
      I shook the pillaring hours
And pulled my life upon me; grimed with smears,
I stand amid the dust o' the mounded years—
My mangled youth lies dead beneath the heap.
My days have cracked and gone up in smoke,
Have puffed and burst as sun-starts on a stream.
      Yea, faileth now even dream

[14]

The dreamer, and the lute the lutanist;
Even the linked fantasies, in whose blossomy twist
I swung the earth a trinket at my wrist,
Are yielding; cords of all too weak account
For earth with heavy griefs so overplussed.
      Ah! is Thy love indeed
A weed, albeit an amaranthine weed,
Suffering no flowers except its own to mount?
      Ah! must—
      Designer infinite!—
Ah! must Thou char the wood ere Thou canst limn with it?
My freshness spent its wavering shower i' the dust;
And now my heart is as a broken fount,
Wherein tear-drippings stagnate, spilt down ever
      From the dank thoughts that shiver
Upon the sighful branches of my mind.
      Such is; what is to be?
The pulp so bitter, how shall taste the rind?
I dimly guess what Time in mists confounds;
Yet ever and anon a trumpet sounds
From the hid battlements of Eternity;
Those shaken mists a space unsettle, then
Round the half-glimpsèd turrets slowly wash again.
      But not ere him who summoneth
      I first have seen, enwound
With glooming robes purpureal, cypress-crowned;
His name I know, and what his trumpet saith.
Whether man's heart or life it be which yields
      Thee harvest, must Thy harvest-fields
      Be dunged with rotten death?
       Now of that long pursuit
       Comes on at hand the bruit;

That Voice is round me like a bursting sea:
   'And is thy earth so marred,
   Shattered in shard on shard?
  Lo, all things fly thee, for thou fliest Me!
  Strange, piteous, futile thing!
Wherefore should any set thee love apart?
Seeing none but I makes much of naught' (He said),
'And human love needs human meriting:
   How hast thou merited—
Of all man's clotted clay the dingiest clot?
   Alack, thou knowest not
How little worthy of any love thou art!
Whom wilt thou find to love ignoble thee,
   Save Me, save only Me?
All which I took from thee I did but take,
   Not for thy harms,
But just that thou might'st seek it in My arms.
   All which thy child's mistake
Fancies as lost, I have stored for thee at home:
   Rise, clasp My hand, and come!'
  Halts by me that footfall:
  Is my gloom, after all,
Shade of His hand, outstretched caressingly?
  'Ah, fondest, blindest, weakest,
  I am He Whom thou seekest!
Thou dravest love from thee, who dravest Me.'

ODE TO THE SETTING SUN

PRELUDE

The wailful sweetness of the violin
  Floats down the hushèd waters of the wind,
The heart-strings of the throbbing harp begin
  To long in aching music.   Spirit-pined,

In wafts that poignant sweetness drifts, until
  The wounded soul ooze sadness.   The red sun,
A bubble of fire, drops slowly toward the hill,
  While one bird prattles that the day is done.

O setting Sun, that as in reverent days
  Sinkest in music to thy smoothèd sleep,
Discrowned of homage, though yet crowned with rays,
  Hymned not at harvest more, though reapers reap:

For thee this music wakes not.   O deceived,
  If thou hear in these thoughtless harmonies
A pious phantom of adorings reaved,
  And echo of fair ancient flatteries!

Yet, in this field where the Cross planted reigns,
  I know not what strange passion bows my head
To thee, whose great command upon my veins
  Proves thee a god for me not dead, not dead!

For worship it is too incredulous,
  For doubt—oh, too believing-passionate!
What wild divinity makes my heart thus
  A fount of most baptismal tears?—Thy straight

[17]

Long gleam lies steady on the Cross. Ah me!
    What secret would thy radiant finger show?
Of the bright mastership is this the key?
    Is *this* thy secret, then? And is it woe?

Fling from thine ear the burning curls, and hark
    A song thou hast not heard in Northern day;
For Rome too daring, and for Greece too dark,
    Sweet with wild things that pass, that pass away!

ODE

Alpha and Omega, sadness and mirth,
    The springing music, and its wasting breath—
The fairest things in life are Death and Birth,
    And of these two the fairer thing is Death.
Mystical twins of Time inseparable,
    The younger hath the holier array,
        And hath the awfuller sway:
    It is the falling star that trails the light,
    It is the breaking wave that hath the might,
The passing shower that rainbows maniple.
    Is it not so, O thou down-stricken Day,
That draw'st thy splendours round thee in thy fall?
High was thine Eastern pomp inaugural;
But thou dost set in statelier pageantry,
    Lauded with tumults of a firmament:
Thy visible music-blasts make deaf the sky,
    Thy cymbals clang to fire the Occident,
Thou dost thy dying so triumphally:
I *see* the crimson blaring of thy shawms!
        Why doth those lucent palms

[18]

Strew thy feet's failing thicklier than their might,
Who dost but hood thy glorious eyes with night,
And vex the heels of all the yesterdays?
          Lo! this loud, lackeying praise
Will stay behind to greet the usurping moon,
     When they have cloud-barred over thee the West.
Oh, shake the bright dust from thy parting shoon!
     The earth not paeans thee, nor serves thy hest;
Be godded not by Heaven! avert thy face,
          And leave to blank disgrace
The oblivious world! unsceptre thee of state and place!

Ha! but bethink thee what thou gazedst on,
     Ere yet the snake Decay had venomed tooth;
The name thou bar'st in those vast seasons gone—
          Candid Hyperion,
     Clad in the light of thine immortal youth!
          Ere Dionysus bled thy vines,
Or Artemis drave her clamours through the wood,
     Thou saw'st how once against Olympus' height
          The brawny Titans stood,
And shook the gods' world 'bout their ears, and how
Enceladus (whom Etna cumbers now)
     Shouldered me Pelion with its swinging pines,
The river unrecked, that did its broken flood
Spurt on his back: before the mountainous shock
          The rankèd gods dislock,
Scared to their skies; wide o'er rout-trampled night
Flew spurned the pebbled stars: those splendours then
     Had tempested on earth, star upon star
     Mounded in ruin, if a longer war
Had quaked Olympus and cold-fearing men.

Then did the ample marge
And circuit of thy targe
Sullenly redden of all the vaward fight,
   Above the blusterous clash
   Wheeled thy swung falchion's flash,
And hewed their forces into splintered flight.

Yet ere Olympus thou wast, and a god!
      Though we deny thy nod,
We cannot spoil thee of thy divinity.
      What know we elder than thee?
When thou didst, bursting from the great void's husk,
Leap like a lion on the throat o' the dusk;
      When the angels rose-chapleted
         Sang each to other,
      The vaulted blaze overhead
      Of their vast pinions spread,
         Hailing thee brother;
How chaos rolled back from the wonder,
And the First Morn knelt down to thy visage of thunder!
      Thou didst draw to thy side
      Thy young Auroral bride,
   And lift her veil of night and mystery;
      Tellus with baby hands
      Shook off her swaddling-bands,
And from the unswathèd vapours laughed to thee.

Thou twi-form deity, nurse at once and sire!
   Thou genitor that all things nourishest!
   The earth was suckled at thy shining breast,
And in her veins is quick thy milky fire.

Who scarfed her with the morning? and who set
Upon her brow the day-fall's carcanet?
  Who queened her front with the enrondured moon?
    Who dug night's jewels from their vaulty mine
      To dower her, past an eastern wizard's dreams,
  When, hovering on him through his haschish-swoon,
    All the rained gems of the old Tartarian line
Shiver in lustrous throbbings of tinged flame?
      Whereof a moiety in the Paolis' seams
      Statelily builded their Venetian name.
        Thou hast enwoofèd her
        An empress of the air,
And all her births are propertied by thee:
        Her teeming centuries
        Drew being from thine eyes:
Thou fatt'st the marrow of all quality.

Who lit the furnace of the mammoth's heart?
  Who shagged him like Pilatus' ribbèd flanks?
    Who raised the columned ranks
Of that old pre-diluvian forestry,
Which like a continent torn oppressed the sea,
  When the ancient heavens did in rains depart,
    While the high-dancèd whirls
Of the tossed scud made hiss thy drenchèd curls?
    Thou rear'dst the enormous brood;
  Who hast with life imbued
The lion maned in tawny majesty,
    The tiger velvet-barred,
    The stealthy-stepping pard,
And the lithe panther's flexous symmetry?

[21]

How came the entombèd tree a light-bearer,
        Though sunk in lightless lair?
        Friend of the forgers of earth,
    Mate of the earthquake and thunders volcanic,
    Clasped in the arms of the forces Titanic
        Which rock like a cradle the girth
            Of the ether-hung world;
    Swart son of the swarthy mine,
    When flame on the breath of his nostrils feeds
    How is his countenance half-divine,
    Like thee in thy sanguine weeds?
        Thou gavest him his light,
        Though sepultured in night
Beneath the dead bones of a perished world;
        Over his prostrate form
        Though cold, and heat, and storm,
The mountainous wrack of a creation hurled.

        Who made the splendid rose
        Saturate with purple glows;
Cupped to the marge with beauty; a perfume-press
        Whence the wind vintages
Gushes of warmèd fragrance richer far
    Than all the flavorous ooze of Cyprus' vats?
Lo, in yon gale which waves her green cymar,
        With dusky cheeks burnt red
        She sways her heavy head,
Drunk with the must of her own odorousness;
    While in a moted trouble the vexed gnats
Maze, and vibrate, and tease the noontide hush.
    Who girt dissolvèd lightnings in the grape?
Summered the opal with an Irised flush?

[22]

Is it not thou that dost the tulip drape,
    And huest the daffodilly,
    Yet who has snowed the lily,
And her frail sister, whom the waters name,
    Dost vestal-vesture 'mid the blaze of June,
    Cold as the new-sprung girlhood of the moon
Ere Autumn's kiss sultry her cheek with flame?
    Thou sway'st thy sceptred beam
    O'er all delight and dream,
    Beauty is beautiful but in thy glance:
        And like a jocund maid
        In garland-flowers arrayed,
    Before thy ark Earth keeps her sacred dance.

And now, O shaken from thine antique throne,
    And sunken from thy coerule empery,
Now that the red glare of thy fall is blown
    In smoke and flame about the windy sky,
Where are the wailing voices that should meet
    From hill, stream, grove, and all of mortal shape
Who tread thy gifts, in vineyards as stray feet
    Pulp the gloved weight of juiced Iberia's grape?
        Where is the threne o' the sea?
        And why not dirges thee
The wind, that sings to himself as he makes stride
    Lonely and terrible on the Andèan height?
        Where is the Naiad 'mid her sworded sedge?
    The Nymph wan-glimmering by her wan fount's verge?
The Dryad at timid gaze by the wood-side?
        The Oread jutting light
    On one up-strainèd sole from the rock-ledge?
        The Nereid tip-toe on the scud o' the surge,

[23]

With whistling tresses dank athwart her face,
And all her figure poised in lithe Circean grace?
　　　Why withers their lament?
　　　Their tresses tear-besprent,
　　Have they sighed hence with trailing garment-hem?
　　　O sweet, O sad, O fair,
　　　I catch your flying hair,
　　Draw your eyes down to me, and dream on them!

A space, and they fleet from me. Must ye fade—
O old, essential candours, ye who made
　　The earth a living and a radiant thing—
　　　And leave her corpse in our strained, cheated arms?
　　　Lo ever thus, when Song with chorded charms
Draws from dull death his lost Eurydice,
　　Lo ever thus, even at consummating,
　　Even in the swooning minute that claims her his,
　　Of reincarnate Beauty, his control
　　Clasps the cold body, and foregoes the soul!
　　　Whatso looks lovelily
Is but the rainbow on life's weeping rain.
Why have we longings of immortal pain,
And all we long for mortal? Woe is me,
And all our chants but chaplet some decay,
As mine this vanishing—nay, vanished Day.
The low sky-line dusks to a leaden hue,
　　No rift disturbs the heavy shade and chill,
Save one, where the charred firmament lets through
　　The scorching dazzle of Heaven; 'gainst which the hill,
　　　Out-flattened sombrely,
Stands black as life against eternity.
　　　Against eternity?

A rifting light in me
Burns through the leaden broodings of the mind:
O blessèd Sun, thy state
Uprisen or derogate
Dafts me no more with doubt; I seek and find.
If with exultant tread
Thou foot the Eastern sea,
Or like a golden bee
Sting the West to angry red,
Thou dost image, thou dost follow
That King-Maker of Creation,
Who, ere Hellas hailed Apollo,
Gave thee, angel-god, thy station;
Thou art of Him a type memorial.
Like him thou hang'st in dreadful pomp of blood
Upon thy Western rood;
And His stained brow did vail like thine to night,
Yet lift once more Its light,
And, risen, again departed from our ball,
But when It set on earth arose in Heaven.
Thus hath He unto death His beauty given:
And so of all which form inheriteth
The fall doth pass the rise in worth;
For birth hath in itself the germ of death,
But death hath in itself the germ of birth.
It is the falling acorn buds the tree,
The falling rain that bears the greenery,
The fern-plants moulder when the ferns arise.
For there is nothing lives but something dies,
And there is nothing dies but something lives.
Till skies be fugitives,
Till Time, the hidden root of change, updries,

Are Birth and Death inseparable on earth;
For they are twain yet one, and Death is Birth.

AFTER-STRAIN

Now with wan ray that other sun of Song
    Sets in the bleakening waters of my soul:
One step, and lo! the Cross stands gaunt and long
    'Twixt me and yet bright skies, a presaged dole.

Even so, O Cross! thine is the victory.
    Thy roots are fast within our fairest fields;
Brightness may emanate in Heaven from thee,
    Here thy dread symbol only shadow yields.

Of reapèd joys thou art the heavy sheaf
    Which must be lifted, though the reaper groan;
Yea, we may cry till Heaven's great ear be deaf,
    But we must bear thee, and must bear alone.

Vain were a Simon; of the Antipodes
    Our night not borrows the superfluous day.
Yet woe to him that from his burden flees,
    Crushed in the fall of what he cast away.

Therefore, O tender Lady, Queen Mary,
    Thou gentleness that dost enmoss and drape
The Cross's rigorous austerity,
    Wipe thou the blood from wounds that needs must gape.

'Lo, though suns rise and set, but crosses stay,
    I leave thee ever,' saith she, 'light of cheer.'
'Tis so: yon sky still thinks upon the Day,
    And showers aërial blossoms on his bier.

Yon cloud with wrinkled fire is edgèd sharp;
  And once more welling through the air, ah me!
How the sweet viol plains him to the harp,
  Whose pangèd sobbings throng tumultuously.

Oh, this Medusa-pleasure with her stings!
  This essence of all suffering, which is joy!
I am not thankless for the spell it brings,
  Though tears must be told down for the charmed toy.

No; while soul, sky, and music bleed together,
  Let me give thanks even for those griefs in me,
The restless windward stirrings of whose feather
  Prove them the brood of immortality.

My soul is quitted of death-neighbouring swoon,
  Who shall not slake her immitigable scars
Until she hear 'My sister!' from the moon,
  And take the kindred kisses of the stars.

Ī

THE VETERAN OF HEAVEN

O Captain of the wars, whence won Ye so great scars?
  In what fight did Ye smite, and what manner was the foe?
Was it on a day of rout they compassed Thee about,
    Or gat Ye these adornings when Ye wrought their over-
      throw?

' 'Twas on a day of rout they girded Me about,
    They wounded all My brow, and they smote Me through
      the side:
My hand held no sword when I met their armèd horde,
    And the conqueror fell down, and the Conquered bruised
      his pride.'

What is this, unheard before, that the Unarmed makes war,
    And the Slain hath the gain, and the Victor hath the rout?
What wars, then, are these, and what the enemies,
    Strange Chief, with the scars of Thy conquest trenched
      about?

'The Prince I drave forth held the Mount of the North,
    Girt with the guards of flame that roll round the pole.
I drave him with My wars from all his fortress-stars,
    And the sea of death divided that My march might strike
      its goal.

[28]

'In the heart of Northern Guard, many a great dæmonian
      sword
    Burns as it turns round the Mount occult, apart:
There is given him power and place still for some certain
      days,
    And his name would turn the Sun's blood back upon its
      heart.'

What is *Thy* Name? Oh, show!—'My Name ye may not
      know;
    'Tis a going forth with banners, and a baring of much
      swords:
But My titles that are high, are they not upon My thigh?
    "King of Kings!" are the words, "Lord of Lords!"
    It is written "King of Kings, Lord of Lords." '

II

LILIUM REGIS

O Lily of the King! low lies thy silver wing,
    And long has been the hour of thine unqueening;
And thy scent of Paradise on the night-wind spills its sighs,
    Nor any take the secrets of its meaning.
O Lily of the King! I speak a heavy thing,
    O patience, most sorrowful of daughters!
Lo, the hour is at hand for the troubling of the land,
    And red shall be the breaking of the waters.

Sit fast upon thy stalk, when the blast shall with thee talk,
    With the mercies of the King for thine awning;
And the just understand that thine hour is at hand,
    Thine hour at hand with power in the dawning.

[29]

When the nations lie in blood, and their kings a broken
    brood,
  Look up, O most sorrowful of daughters!
Lift up thy head and hark what sounds are in the dark,
  For His feet are coming to thee on the waters!

O Lily of the King! I shall not see, that sing,
  I shall not see the hour of thy queening!
But my Song shall see, and wake like a flower that dawn-
    winds shake,
  And sigh with joy the odours of its meaning.
O Lily of the King, remember then the thing
  That this dead mouth sang; and thy daughters,
As they dance before His way, sing there on the Day
  What I sang when the Night was on the waters!

THE MISTRESS OF VISION

I

SECRET was the garden;
Set i' the pathless awe
Where no star its breath can draw.
Life, that is its warden,
Sits behind the fosse of death.   Mine eyes saw not, and I
saw.

II

It was a mazeful wonder;
Thrice three times it was enwalled
With an emerald—
Sealèd so asunder.
All its birds in middle air hung a-dream, their music thralled.

III

The Lady of fair weeping,
At the garden's core,
Sang a song of sweet and sore
And the after-sleeping;
In the land of Luthany, and the tracts of Elenore.

IV

With sweet-pangèd singing,
Sang she through a dream-night's day;
That the bowers might stay,
Birds bate their winging,
Nor the wall of emerald float in wreathèd haze away.

V

The lily kept its gleaming,
In her tears (divine conservers!)
Washèd with sad art;
And the flowers of dreaming
Palèd not their fervours,
For her blood flowed through their nervures;
And the roses were most red, for she dipt them in her heart.

VI

There was never moon,
Save the white sufficing woman:
Light most heavenly-human—
Like the unseen form of sound,
Sensed invisibly in tune,—
With a sun-derivèd stole
Did inaureole
All her lovely body round;
Lovelily her lucid body with that light was interstrewn.

VII

The sun which lit that garden wholly,
Low and vibrant visible,
Tempered glory woke;
And it seemèd solely
Like a silver thurible
Solemnly swung, slowly,
Fuming clouds of golden fire, for a cloud of incense-smoke.

VIII

But woe's me, and woe's me,
For the secrets of her eyes!
In my visions fearfully
They are ever shown to be
As fringèd pools, whereof each lies
Pallid-dark beneath the skies
Of a night that is
But one blear necropolis.
And her eyes a little tremble, in the wind of her own sighs.

IX

Many changes rise on
Their phantasmal mysteries.
They grow to an horizon
Where earth and heaven meet;
And like a wing that dies on
The vague twilight-verges,
Many a sinking dream doth fleet
Lessening down their secrecies.
And, as dusk with day converges,
Their orbs are troublously
Over-gloomed and over-glowed with hope and fear of things
    to be.

X

There is a peak on Himalay,
And on the peak undeluged snow,
And on the snow not eagles stray;
There if your strong feet could go,—
Looking over tow'rd Cathay
From the never-deluged snow—
Farthest ken might not survey
Where the peoples underground dwell whom antique fables
know.

XI

East, ah, east of Himalay,
Dwell the nations underground;
Hiding from the shock of Day,
For the sun's uprising-sound:
Dare not issue from the ground
At the tumults of the Day,
So fearfully the sun doth sound
Clanging up beyond Cathay;
For the great earthquaking sunrise rolling up beyond
Cathay.

XII

Lend me, O lend me
The terrors of that sound,
That its music may attend me,
Wrap my chant in thunders round;
While I tell the ancient secrets in that Lady's singing found.

XIII

On Ararat there grew a vine;
When Asia from her bathing rose,
Our first sailor made a twine
Thereof for his prefiguring brows.
Canst divine
Where, upon our dusty earth, of that vine a cluster grows?

XIV

On Golgotha there grew a thorn
Round the long-prefigured Brows.
Mourn, O mourn!
For the vine have we the spine? Is this all the Heaven
allows?

XV

On Calvary was shook a spear;
Press the point into thy heart—
Joy and fear!
All the spines upon the thorn into curling tendrils start.

XVI

O dismay!
I, a wingless mortal, sporting
With the tresses of the sun?
On the thunder in its snorting?
Ere begun,
Falls my singed song down the sky, even the old Icarian
way.

XVII

From the fall precipitant
These dim snatches of her chant
Only have remainèd mine;—
That from spear and thorn alone
May be grown
For the front of saint or singer any divinizing twine.

XVIII

Her song said that no springing
Paradise but evermore
Hangeth on a singing
That has chords of weeping,
And that sings the after-sleeping
To souls which wake too sore.
'But woe the singer, woe!' she said; 'beyond the dead his
singing-lore,
All its art of sweet and sore,
He learns, in Elenore!'

XIX

Where is the land of Luthany,
Where is the tract of Elenore?
I am bound therefor.

'Pierce thy heart to find the key;
With thee take
Only what none else would keep;
Learn to dream when thou dost wake,
Learn to wake when thou dost sleep;
Learn to water joy with tears,
Learn from fears to vanquish fears,
To hope, for thou dar'st not despair,
Exult, for that thou dar'st not grieve;
Plough thou the rock until it bear;
Know, for thou else couldst not believe;
Lose, that the lost thou may'st receive;
Die, for none other way canst live.
When earth and heaven lay down their veil,
And that apocalypse turns thee pale;
When thy seeing blindeth thee
To what thy fellow-mortals see;
When their sight to thee is sightless;
Their living, death; their light, most lightless;
Search no more—
Pass the gates of Luthany, tread the region Elenore.'

XXI

Where is the land of Luthany,
And where the region Elenore?
I do faint therefor.

'When to the new eyes of thee
All things by immortal power,
Near or far,
Hiddenly
To each other linkèd are,
That thou canst not stir a flower
Without troubling of a star;
When thy song is shield and mirror
To the fair snake-curlèd Pain,
Where thou dar'st affront her terror
That on her thou may'st attain
Perséan conquest; seek no more,
O seek no more!
Pass the gates of Luthany, tread the region Elenore.'

XXIII

So sang she, so wept she,
Through a dream-night's day;
And with her magic singing kept she—
Mystical in music—
That garden of enchanting
In visionary May;
Swayless for my spirit's haunting,
Thrice-threefold walled with emerald from our mortal mornings grey.

XXIV

And as a necromancer
Raises from the rose-ash
The ghost of the rose;
My heart so made answer
To her voice's silver plash,—
Stirred in reddening flash,
And from out its mortal ruins the purpureal phantom blows.

XXV

Her tears made dulcet fretting,
Her voice had no word,
More than thunder or the bird.
Yet, unforgetting,
The ravished soul her meanings knew.   Mine ears heard
   not, and I heard.

XXVI

When she shall unwind
All those wiles she wound about me,
Tears shall break from out me,
That I cannot find
Music in the holy poets to my wistful want, I doubt me!

AN ANTHEM OF EARTH

PROEMION

IMMEASURABLE Earth!
Through the loud vast and populacy of Heaven,
Tempested with gold schools of ponderous orbs,
That cleav'st with deep-revolving harmonies
Passage perpetual, and behind thee draw'st
A furrow sweet, a cometary wake
Of trailing music! What large effluence,
Not sole the cloudy sighing of thy seas,
Nor thy blue-coifing air, encases thee
From prying of the stars, and the broad shafts
Of thrusting sunlight tempers? For, dropped near
From my removèd tour in the serene
Of utmost contemplation, I scent lives.
This is the efflux of thy rocks and fields,
And wind-cuffed forestage, and the souls of men,
And aura of all treaders over thee;
A sentient exhalation, wherein close
The odorous lives of many-throated flowers,
And each thing's mettle effused; that so thou wear'st,
Even like a breather on a frosty morn,
Thy proper suspiration. For I know,
Albeit, with custom-dulled perceivingness,
Nestled against thy breast, my sense not take
The breathings of thy nostrils, there's no tree,
No grain of dust, nor no cold-seeming stone,
But wears a fume of its circumfluous self.
Thine own life and the lives of all that live,
The issue of thy loins,
Is this thy gabardine,

Wherein thou walkest through thy large demesne
And sphery pleasances,—
Amazing the unstalèd eyes of Heaven,
And us that still a precious seeing have
Behind this dim and mortal jelly.

Ah!

If not in all too late and frozen a day
I come in rearward of the throats of song,
Unto the deaf sense of the agèd year
Singing with doom upon me; yet give heed!
One poet with sick pinion, that still feels
Breath through the Orient gateways closing fast,
Fast closing t'ward the undelighted night!

ANTHEM

In nescientness, in nescientness,
Mother, we put these fleshly lendings on
Thou yield'st to thy poor children; took thy gift
Of life, which must, in all the after days,
Be craved again with tears,—
With fresh and still-petitionary tears.
Being once bound thine almsmen for that gift,
We are bound to beggary, nor our own can call
The journal dole of customary life,
But after suit obsequious for't to thee.
Indeed this flesh, O Mother,
A beggar's gown, a client's badging,
We find, which from thy hands we simply took,
Naught dreaming of the after penury,
In nescientness.
In a little joy, in a little joy,

We wear awhile thy sore insignia,
Nor know thy heel o' the neck. O Mother! Mother!
Then what use knew I of thy solemn robes,
But as a child to play with them? I bade thee
Leave thy great husbandries, thy grave designs,
Thy tedious state which irked my ignorant years,
Thy winter-watches, suckling of the grain,
Severe premeditation taciturn
Upon the brooded Summer, thy chill cares,
And all thy ministries majestical,
To sport with me, thy darling. Thought I not
Thou sett'st thy seasons forth processional
To pamper me with pageant,—thou thyself
My fellow-gamester, appanage of mine arms?
Then what wild Dionysia I, young Bacchanal,
Danced in thy lap! Ah for thy gravity!
Then, O Earth, thou rang'st beneath me,
Rocked to Eastward, rocked to Westward,
Even with the shifted
Poise and footing of my thought!
I brake through thy doors of sunset,
Ran before the hooves of sunrise,
Shook thy matron tresses down in fancies
Wild and wilful
As a poet's hand could twine them;
Caught in my fantasy's crystal chalice
The Bow, as its cataract of colours
Plashed to thee downward;
Then when thy circuit swung to nightward,
Night the abhorrèd, night was a new dawning,
Celestial dawning
Over the ultimate marges of the soul;
Dusk grew turbulent with fire before me,

And like a windy arras waved with dreams.
Sleep I took not for my bedfellow,
Who could waken
To a revel, an inexhaustible
Wassail of orgiac imageries;
Then while I wore thy sore insignia
In a little joy, O Earth, in a little joy;
Loving thy beauty in all creatures born of thee,
Children, and the sweet-essenced body of woman;
Feeling not yet upon my neck thy foot,
But breathing warm of thee as infants breathe
New from their mother's morning bosom. So I,
Risen from thee, restless winnower of the heaven,
Most Hermes-like, did keep
My vital and resilient path, and felt
The play of wings about my fledgèd heel—
Sure on the verges of precipitous dream,
Swift in its springing
From jut to jut of inaccessible fancies,
In a little joy.

In a little thought, in a little thought,
We stand and eye thee in a grave dismay
With sad and doubtful questioning, when first
Thou speak'st to us as men: like sons who hear
Newly their mother's history, unthought
Before, and say—'She is not as we dreamed:
Ah me! we are beguiled!' What art thou, then,
That art not our conceiving? Art thou not
Too old for thy young children? Or perchance,
Keep'st thou a youth perpetual-burnishable
Beyond thy sons decrepit? It is long

Since Time was first a fledgeling;
Yet thou may'st be but as a pendant bulla
Against his stripling bosom swung. Alack!
For that we seem indeed
To have slipped the world's great leaping-time, and come
Upon thy pinched and dozing days: these weeds,
These corporal leavings, thou not cast'st us new
Fresh from thy craftship, like the lilies' coats,
But foist'st us off
With hasty tarnished piecings negligent,
Snippets and waste
From old ancestral wearings,
That have seen sorrier usage; remainder-flesh
After our father's surfeits; nay with chinks,
Some of us, that, if speech may have free leave,
Our souls go out at elbows. We are sad
With more than our sires' heaviness, and with
More than weakness weak; we shall not be
Mighty with all their mightiness, nor shall not
Rejoice with all their joy. Ay, Mother! Mother!
What is this Man, thy darling kissed and cuffed,
Thou lustingly engender'st,
To sweat, and make his brag, and rot,
Crowned with all honour and all shamefulness?
From nightly towers
He dogs the secret footsteps of the heavens,
Sifts in his hands the stars, weighs them as gold-dust,
And yet is he successive unto nothing
But patrimony of a little mold,
And entail of four planks. Thou hast made his mouth
Avid of all dominion and all mightiness,
All sorrow, all delight, all topless grandeurs,

All beauty, and all starry majesties,
And dim transtellar things;—even that it may,
Filled in the ending with a puff of dust,
Confess—'It is enough.' The world left empty
What that poor mouthful crams. His heart builded
For pride, for potency, infinity,
All heights, all deeps, and all immensities,
Arrased with purple like the house of kings,—
To stall the grey-rat, and the carrion-worm
Statelily lodge. Mother of mysteries!
Sayer of dark sayings in a thousand tongues,
Who bringest forth no saying yet so dark
As we ourselves, thy darkest! We the young,
In a little thought, in a little thought,
At last confront thee, and ourselves in thee,
And wake disgarmented of glory: as one
On a mount standing, and against him stands,
On the mount adverse, crowned with westering rays,
The golden sun, and they two brotherly
Gaze each on each;
He faring down
To the dull vale, his Godhead peels from him
Till he can scarcely spurn the pebble—
For nothingness of new-found mortality—
That mutinies against his gallèd foot.
Littly he sets him to the daily way,
With all around the valleys growing grave,
And known things changed and strange; but he holds on,
Though all the land of light be widowèd,
In a little thought.

In a little strength, in a little strength,
We affront thy unveiled face intolerable,

Which yet we do sustain.
Though I the Orient never more shall feel
Break like a clash of cymbals, and my heart
Clang through my shaken body like a gong;
Nor ever more with spurted feet shall tread
I' the winepresses of song; naught's truly lost
That moulds to sprout forth gain: now I have on me
The high Phœbean priesthood, and that craves
An unrash utterance; not with flaunted hem
May the Muse enter in behind the veil,
Nor, though we hold the sacred dances good,
Shall the holy Virgins mænadize: ruled lips
Befit a votaress Muse.
Thence with no mutable, nor no gelid love,
I keep, O Earth, thy worship,
Though life slow, and the sobering Genius change
To a lamp his gusty torch. What though no more
Athwart its roseal glow
Thy face look forth triumphal? Thou putt'st on
Strange sanctities of pathos; like this knoll
Made derelict of day,
Couchant and shadowèd
Under dim Vesper's overloosened hair:
This, where embossèd with the half-blown seed
The solemn purple thistle stands in grass
Grey as an exhalation, when the bank
Holds mist for water in the nights of Fall.
Not to the boy, although his eyes be pure
As the prime snowdrop is
Ere the rash Phœbus break her cloister
Of sanctimonious snow;
Or Winter fasting sole on Himalay

Since those dove-nuncioed days
When Asia rose from bathing;
Not to such eyes,
Uneuphrasied with tears, the hierarchical
Vision lies unoccult, rank under rank
Through all create down-wheeling, from the Throne
Even to the bases of the pregnant ooze.
This is the enchantment, this the exaltation,
The all-compensating wonder,
Giving to common things wild kindred
With the gold-tesserate floors of Jove;
Linking such heights and such humilities
Hand in hand in ordinal dances,
That I do think my tread,
Stirring the blossoms in the meadow-grass,
Flickers the unwithering stars.
This to the shunless fardel of the world
Nerves my uncurbèd back: that I endure,
The monstrous Temple's moveless caryatid,
With wide eyes calm upon the whole of things,
In a little strength.

In a little sight, in a little sight,
We learn from what in thee is credible
The incredible, with bloody clutch and feet
Clinging the painful juts of jaggèd faith.
Science, old noser in its prideful straw,
That with anatomising scalpel tents
Its three-inch of thy skin, and brags 'All's bare'—
The eyeless worm, that, boring, works the soil,
Making it capable for the crops of God;
Against its own dull will
Ministers poppies to our troublous thought,

A Balaam come to prophecy,—parables,
Nor of its parable itself is ware,
Grossly unwotting; all things has expounded,
Reflux and influx, counts the sepulchre
The seminary of being, and extinction
The Ceres of existence: it discovers
Life in putridity, vigour in decay;
Dissolution even, and disintegration,
Which in our dull thoughts symbolize disorder
Finds in God's thoughts irrefragable order,
And admirable the manner of our corruption
As of our health. It grafts upon the cypress
The tree of Life—Death dies on his own dart
Promising to our ashes perpetuity,
And to our perishable elements
Their proper imperishability; extracting
Medicaments from out mortality
Against too mortal cogitation; till
Even of the *caput mortuum* we do thus
Make a *memento vivere*. To such uses
I put the blinding knowledge o' the fool,
Who in no order seeth ordinance;
Nor thrust my arm in nature shoulder-high,
And cry—'There's naught beyond!' How should I so,
That cannot with these arms of mine engirdle
All which I am; that am a foreigner
In mine own region? Who the chart shall draw
Of the strange courts and vaulty labyrinths,
The spacious tenements and wide pleasances,
Innumerable corridors far-withdrawn,
Wherein I wander darkling, of myself?
Darkling I wander, nor I dare explore

The long arcane of those dim catacombs,
Where the rat memory does its burrows make,
Close-seal them as I may, and my stolen tread
Starts populace, a *gens lucifuga;*
That too strait seems my mind my mind to hold,
And I myself incontinent of me.
Then go I, my foul-venting ignorance
With scabby sapience plastered, aye forsooth!
Clap my wise foot-rule to the walls o' the world,
And vow—*A goodly house, but something ancient,*
And I can find no Master?   Rather, nay,
By baffled seeing, something I divine
Which baffles, and a seeing set beyond;
And so with strenuous gazes sounding down,
Like to the day-long porer on a stream,
Whose last look is his deepest, I beside
This slow perpetual Time stand patiently,
In a little sight.

In a little dust, in a little dust,
Earth, thou reclaim'st us, who do all our lives
Find of thee but Egyptian villeinage.
Thou dost his body, this enhavocked realm,
Subject to ancient and ancestral shadows;
Descended passions sway it; it is distraught
With ghostly usurpation, dinned and fretted
With the still-tyrannous dead; a haunted tenement,
Peopled from barrows and outworn ossuaries.
Thou giv'st us life not half so willingly
As thou undost thy giving; thou that teem'st
The stealthy terror of the sinuous pard,
The lion maned with curlèd puissance,
The serpent, and all fair strong beasts of ravin,

Thyself most fair and potent beast of ravin,
And thy great eaters thou, the greatest, eat'st.
Thou hast devoured mammoth and mastodon,
And many a floating bank of fangs,
The scaly scourges of thy primal brine,
And the tower-crested plesiosaure.
Thou fill'st thy mouth with nations, gorgest slow
On purple æons of kings; man's hulking towers
Are carcase for thee, and to modern sun
Disglutt'st their splintered bones.
Rabble of Pharaohs and Arsacidæ
Keep their cold house within thee; thou hast sucked down
How many Ninevehs and Hecatompyloi,
And perished cities whose great phantasmata
O'erbrow the silent citizens of Dis:—
Hast not thy fill?
Tarry awhile, lean Earth, for thou shalt drink,
Even till thy dull throat sicken,
The draught thou grow'st most fat on; hear'st thou not
The world's knives bickering in their sheaths?   O pa-
    tience!
Much offal of a foul world comes thy way,
And man's superfluous cloud shall soon be laid
In a little blood.

In a little peace, in a little peace,
Thou dost rebate thy rigid purposes
Of imposed being, and relenting, mend'st
Too much, with naught. The westering Phœbus' horse
Paws i' the lucent dust as when he shocked
The East with rising; O how may I trace
In this decline that morning when we did

[50]

Sport 'twixt the claws of newly-whelped existence,
Which had not yet learned rending? We did then
Divinely stand, not knowing yet against us
Sentence had passed of life, nor commutation
Petitioning into death. What's he that of
The Free State argues? Tellus, bid him stoop,
Even where the low *hic jacet* answers him;
Thus low, O Man! there's freedom's seignory,
Tellus' most reverend sole free commonweal,
And model deeply-policied: there none
Stands on precedence, nor ambitiously
Woos the impartial worm, whose favour kiss
With liberal largesse all; there each is free
To be e'en what he must, which here did strive
So much to be he could not; there all do
Their uses just, with no flown questioning.
To be took by the hand of equal earth
They doff her livery, slip to the worm,
Which lacqueys them, their suits of maintenance,
And, that soiled workaday apparel cast,
Put on condition: Death's ungentle buffet
Alone makes ceremonial manumission;
So are the heavenly statutes set, and those
Uranian tables of the primal law.
In a little peace, in a little peace,
Like fierce beasts that a common thirst makes brothers,
We draw together to one hid dark lake;
In a little peace, in a little peace,
We drain with all our burthens of dishonour
Into the cleansing sands o' the thirsty grave.
The fiery pomps, brave exhalations,
And all the glistering shows o' the seeming world,

Which the sight aches at, we unwinking see
Through the smoked glass of Death; Death, where-
	with's fined
The muddy wine of life; that earth doth purge
Of her plethora of man; Death, that doth flush
The cumbered gutters of humanity;
Nothing, of nothing king, with front uncrowned,
Whose hand holds crownets; playmate swart o' the strong;
Tenebrous moon that flux and refluence draws
Of the high-tided man; skull-housèd asp
That stings the heel of kings; true Fount of Youth,
Where he that dips is deathless; being's drone-pipe;
Whose nostril turns to blight the shrivelled stars,
And thicks the lusty breathing of the sun;
Pontifical Death, that doth the crevasse bridge
To the steep and the trifid God; one mortal birth
That broker is of immortality.
Under this dreadful brother uterine,
This kinsman feared, Tellus, behold me come,
Thy son stern-nursed; who mortal-motherlike,
To turn thy weanlings' mouth averse, embitter'st
Thine over-childed breast. Now, mortal-sonlike,
I thou hast suckled, Mother, I at last
Shall sustenant be to thee. Here I untrammel,
Here I pluck loose the body's cementing,
And break the tomb of life; here I shake off
The bur o' the world, man's congregation shun,
And to the antique order of the dead
I take the tongueless vows: my cell is set
Here in thy bosom; my trouble is ended
In a little peace.

SONNETS

AD AMICAM

I

DEAR Dove, that bear'st to my sole-labouring ark
   The olive-branch of so long wishèd rest,
When the white solace glimmers through my dark
   Of nearing wings, what comfort in my breast!
Oh, may that doubted day not come, not come,
   When you shall fail, my heavenly messenger,
And drift into the distance and the doom
   Of all my impermissible things that were!
Rather than so, now make the sad farewell,
   Which yet may be with not too-painèd pain,
Lest I again the acquainted tale should tell
   Of sharpest loss that pays for shortest gain.
      Ah, if my heart should hear no white wings thrill
      Against its waiting window, open still!

II*

When from the blossoms of the noiseful day
   Unto the hive of sleep and hushèd gloom
Throng the dim-wingèd dreams are they
   That with the wildest honey hover home?

* Both in its theme and in its imagery this sonnet was written as a variation
of Mrs. Meynell's verses 'At Night.'

[53]

Oh, they that have from many thousand thoughts
    Stolen the strange sweet of every-blossomy you,
A thousand fancies in fair-coloured knots
    Which you are inexhausted meadow to.
Ah, what sharp heathery honey, quick with pain,
    Do they bring home! It holds the night awake
To hear their lovely murmur in my brain;
    And Sleep's wings have a trouble for your sake.
        Day and you dawn together: for at end
        With the first light breaks the first thought—
          'My friend!'

III

O Friend, who mak'st that mis-spent word of 'friend'
    Sweet as the low note that a summer dove
Fondles in her warm throat! And shall it end,
    Because so swift on friend and friend broke love?
Lo, when all words to honour thee are spent,
    And flung a bold stave to the old bald Time
Telling him that he is too insolent
    Who thinks to rase thee from my heart or rhyme;
Whereof to one because thou life hast given,
    The other yet shall give a life to thee,
Such as to gain, the prowest swords have striven,
    And compassed weaker immortality:
        These spent, my heart not stinteth in her breast
        Her sweet 'Friend! friend!'—one note, and loves
          it best.

IV

No, no, it cannot be, it cannot be,
   Because this love of close-affinèd friends
In its sweet sudden ambush toilèd me
   So swift, that therefore all as swift it ends.
For swift it was, yet quiet as the birth
   Of smoothest Music in a Master's soul,
Whose mild fans lapsing as she slides to earth
   Waver in the bold arms which dare control
Her from her lineal heaven; yea, it was still
   As the young Moon that bares her nightly breast,
And smiles to see the Babe earth suck its fill.
   O Halcyon! was thine auspice not of rest?
     Shall this proud verse bid after-livers see
     How friends could love for immortality?

V

When that part heavenliest of all-heavenly you
   First at my side did breathe its blossomy air,
What lovely wilderment alarmed me through!
   On what ambrosial effluence did I fare,
And comforts Paradisal! What gales came,
   Through ports for one divinest space ajar,
Of rankèd lilies blown into a flame
   By watered banks where walks of young Saints
     are!
One attent space, my trembling locks did rise
   Swayed on the wind, in planetary wheel
Of intervolving sweet societies,
   From wavèd vesture and from fledgèd heel
     Odorous aspersion trailing. Then, alone
     In her eyes' ventral glory, God took throne.

[55]

DESIDERIUM INDESIDERATUM

O Gain that lurk'st ungainèd in all gain!
O love we just fall short of in all love!
O height that in all heights art still above!
O beauty that dost leave all beauty pain!
Thou unpossessed that mak'st possession vain,
See these strained arms which fright the simple air,
And say what ultimate fairness holds thee, Fair!
They girdle Heaven, and girdle Heaven in vain;
They shut, and lo! but shut in their unrest.
Thereat a voice in me that voiceless was:—
'Whom seekest thou through the unmarged arcanum
And not discern'st to thine own bosom prest?'
I looked. My claspèd arms athwart my breast
Framed the august embraces of the Cross.

NON PAX—EXPECTATIO

Hush! 'tis the gap between two lightnings. Room
Is none for peace in this thou callest peace,
This breathing-while wherein the breathings cease,
The pulses sicken, hearkening through the gloom.
Afar the thunders of a coming doom
Ramp on the cowering winds. Lo! at the dread,
Thy heart's tomb yawns and renders up its dead,—
The hopes 'gainst hope embalmèd in its womb.

Canst thou endure, if the pent flood o'erflows?
Who is estated heir to constancy?
Behold, I hardly know if I outlast
The minute underneath whose heel I live;
Yet I endure, have stayed the minute passed,
Perchance may stay the next. Who knows, who knows?

[56]

DAISY

WHERE the thistle lifts a purple crown
   Six foot out of the turf,
And the harebell shakes on the windy hill—
   O breath of the distant surf!—

The hills look over on the South,
   And southward dreams the sea;
And with the sea-breeze hand in hand
   Came innocence and she.

Where 'mid the gorse the raspberry
   Red for the gatherer springs,
Two children did stray and talk
   Wise, idle, childish things.

She listened with big-lipped surprise,
   Breast-deep mid flower and spine:
Her skin was like a grape whose veins
   Runs snow instead of wine.

She knew not those sweet words she spake,
   Nor knew her own sweet way;
But there's never a bird, so sweet a song
   Thronged in whose throat that day.

Oh, there were flowers in Storrington
   On the turf and on the spray;
But the sweetest flower on Sussex hills
   Was the Daisy-flower that day!

Her beauty smoothed earth's furrowed face.
  She gave me tokens three:—
A look, a word of her winsome mouth,
  And a wild raspberry.

A berry red, a guileless look,
  A still word,—strings of sand!
And yet they made my wild, wild heart
  Fly down to her little hand.

For standing artless as the air,
  And candid as the skies,
She took the berries with her hand,
  And the love with her sweet eyes.

The fairest things have fleetest end,
  Their scent survives their close:
But the rose's scent is bitterness
  To him that loved the rose.

She looked a little wistfully,
  Then went her sunshine way:—
The sea's eye had a mist on it,
  And the leaves fell from the day.

She went her unremembering way,
  She went and left in me
The pang of all the partings gone,
  And partings yet to be.

She left me marvelling why my soul
    Was sad that she was glad;
At all the sadness in the sweet,
    The sweetness in the sad.

Still, still I seemed to see her, still
    Look up with soft replies,
And take the berries with her hand,
    And the love with her lovely eyes.

Nothing begins, and nothing ends,
    That is not paid with moan;
For we are born in other's pain,
    And perish in our own.

THE POPPY

To Monica

Summer set lip to earth's bosom bare,
And left the flushed print in a poppy there:
Like a yawn of fire from the grass it came,
And the fanning wind puffed it to flapping flame.

With burnt mouth, red like a lion's, it drank
The blood of the sun as he slaughtered sank,
And dipped its cup in the purpurate shine
When the Eastern conduits ran with wine.

Till it grew lethargied with fierce bliss,
And hot as a swinked gipsy is,
And drowsed in sleepy savageries,
With mouth wide a-pout for a sultry kiss.

[59]

A child and man paced side by side,
Treading the skirts of eventide;
But between the clasp of his hand and hers
Lay, felt not, twenty withered years.

She turned, with the rout of her dusk South hair,
And saw the sleeping gipsy there:
And snatched and snapped it in swift child's whim,
With—'Keep it, long as you live!'—to him.

And his smile, as nymphs from their laving meres,
Trembled up from a bath of tears;
And joy, like a mew sea-rocked apart,
Tossed on the waves of his troubled heart.

For *he* saw what she did not see,
That—as kindled by its own fervency—
The verge shrivelled inward smoulderingly:
And suddenly 'twixt his hand and hers
He knew the twenty withered years—
No flower, but twenty shrivelled years.

'Was never such thing until this hour,'
Low to his heart he said; 'the flower
Of sleep brings wakening to me,
And of oblivion, memory.'

'Was never this thing to me,' he said,
'Though with bruised poppies my feet are red!'
And again to his own heart very low:
'Oh child! I love, for I love and know;

[60]

'But you, who love nor know at all
The diverse chambers in Love's guest-hall,
Where some rise early, few sit long:
In how differing accents hear the throng
His great Pentecostal tongue;

'Who know not love from amity,
Nor my reported self from me;
A fair fit gift is this, meseems,
You give—this withering flower of dreams

'O frankly fickle, and fickly true,
Do you know what the days will do to you?
To your love and you what the days will do.
O frankly fickle, and fickly true?

'You have loved me, Fair, three lives—or day:
'Twill pass with the passing of my face.
But where *I* go, your face goes too,
To watch lest I play false to you.

'I am but, my sweet, your foster-lover,
Knowing well when certain years are over
You vanish from me to another;
Yet I know, and love, like the foster-mother.

'So, frankly fickle, and fickly true!
For my brief life-while I take from you
This token, fair and fit, meseems,
For me—this withering flower of dreams.'

The sleep-flower sways in the wheat its head,
Heavy with dreams, as that with bread;
The goodly grain and the sun-flushed sleeper
The reaper reaps, and Time the reaper.

I hang 'mid men my needless head,
And my fruit is dreams, as theirs is bread:
The goodly men and the sun-hazed sleeper
Time shall reap, but after the reaper
The world shall glean of me, me the sleeper.

Love, love! your flower of withered dream
In leavèd rhyme lies safe, I deem,
Sheltered and shut in a nook of rhyme,
From the reaper man, and his reaper Time.

Love! *I* fall into the claws of Time:
But lasts within a leavèd rhyme
All that the world of me esteems—
My withered dreams, my withered dreams.

TO MONICA THOUGHT DYING

You, O the piteous you!
    Who all the long night through
    Anticipatedly
    Disclose yourself to me
    Already in the ways
Beyond our human comfortable days;
    How can you deem what Death
    Impitiably saith

[62]

To me, who listening wake
For your poor sake?
When a grown woman dies
You know we think unceasingly
What things she said, how sweet, how wise;
And these do make our misery.
But you were (you to me
The dead anticipatedly!)
You—eleven years, was't not, or so?—
Were just a child, you know;
And so you never said
Things sweet immeditatably and wise
To interdict from closure my wet eyes:
But foolish things, my dead, my dead!
Little and laughable,
Your age that fitted well.
And was it such things all unmemorable,
Was it such things could make
Me sob all night for our implacable sake?
Yet, as you said to me,
In pretty make-believe of revelry,
So the night long said Death
With his magniloquent breath;
(And that remembered laughter,
Which in our daily uses followed after,
Was all untuned to pity and to awe:)
    'A cup of chocolate,
    One farthing is the rate,
    You drink it through a straw.'

How could I know, how know
Those laughing words when drenched with sobbing so?
Another voice than yours, he hath.

My dear, was't worth his breath,
His mighty utterance?—yet he saith, and saith!
This dreadful Death to his own dreadfulness
    Doth dreadful wrong,
This dreadful childish babble on his tongue.
That iron tongue made to speak sentences,
And wisdom insupportably complete,
Why should it only say the long night through,
    In mimicry of you,—
    'A cup of chocolate,
    One farthing is the rate,
You drink it through a straw, a straw, a straw!'

    Oh, of all sentences,
    Piercingly incomplete!
Why did you teach that fatal mouth to draw,
    Child, impermissible awe,
    From your old trivialness?
    Why have you done me this
    Most unsustainable wrong,
    And into Death's control
Betrayed the secret places of my soul?—
    Teaching him that his lips,
Uttering their native earthquake and eclipse,
    Could never so avail
To rend from hem to hem the ultimate veil
    Of this most desolate
Spirit, and leave it stripped and desecrate,—
    Nay, never so have wrung
From eyes and speech weakness unmanned, unmeet,
As when his terrible dotage to repeat
Its little lesson learneth at your feet;

As when he sits among
His sepulchres, to play
With broken toys your hand has cast away,
With derelict trinkets of the darling young.
Why have you taught—that he might so complete
His awful panoply
From your cast playthings—why,
This dreadful childish babble to his tongue,
Dreadful and sweet?

THE MAKING OF VIOLA

I

The Father of Heaven.
Spin, daughter Mary, spin,
Twirl your wheel with silver din;
Spin, daughter Mary, spin,
Spin a tress for Viola.

Angels.
Spin, Queen Mary, a
Brown tress for Viola!

II

The Father of Heaven.
Weave, hands angelical,
Weave a woof of flesh to pall—
Weave, hands angelical—
Flesh to pall our Viola.

Angels.
Weave, singing brothers, a
Velvet flesh for Viola!

[65]

III

The Father of Heaven.
> Scoop, young Jesus, for her eyes,
> Wood-browned pools of Paradise—
> Young Jesus, for the eyes,
>> For the eyes of Viola.

Angels.
> Tint, Prince Jesus, a
> Duskèd eye for Viola!

IV

The Father of Heaven.
> Cast a star therein to drown,
> Like a torch in cavern brown,
> Sink a burning star to drown
>> Whelmed in eyes of Viola.

Angels.
> Lave, Prince Jesus, a
> Star in eyes of Viola!

V

The Father of Heaven.
> Breathe, Lord Paraclete,
> To a bubbled crystal meet—
> Breathe, Lord Paraclete—
>> Crystal soul for Viola.

Angels.
> Breathe, Regal Spirit, a
> Flashing soul for Viola!

VI

The Father of Heaven.
>Child-angels, from your wings
>Fall the roseal hoverings,
>Child-angels, from your wings,
>>On the cheeks of Viola.

Angels.
>Linger, rosy reflex, a
>Quenchless stain, on Viola!

VII

All things being accomplished, saith the Father of Heaven:
>Bear her down, and bearing, sing,
>Bear her down on spyless wing,
>Bear her down, and bearing, sing,
>>With a sound of viola.

Angels.
>Music as her name is, a
>Sweet sound of Viola!

VIII

>Wheeling angels, past espial,
>Danced her down with sound of viol;
>Wheeling angels, past espial,
>>Descanting on 'Viola.'

Angels.
>Sing, in our footing, a
>Lovely lilt of 'Viola!'

IX

Baby smiled, mother wailed,
Earthward while the sweetling sailed;
Mother smiled, baby wailed,
    When to earth came Viola.

And her elders shall say:
    So soon have we taught you a
    Way to weep, poor Viola!

X

Smile, sweet baby, smile,
For you will have weeping-while;
Native in your Heaven is smile,—
    But your weeping, Viola?

Whence your smiles we know, but ah!
Whence your weeping, Viola?—
Our first gift to you is a
Gift of tears, my Viola!

TO MY GODCHILD

Francis M. W. M.

This labouring, vast, Tellurian galleon,
Riding at anchor off the orient sun,
Had broken its cable, and stood out to space
Down some frore Arctic of the aërial ways:
And now, back warping from the inclement main,
Its vaporous shroudage drenched with icy rain,
It swung into its azure roads again;

[68]

When, floated on the prosperous sun-gale, you
Lit, a white halcyon auspice, 'mid our frozen crew.
To the Sun, stranger, surely you belong,
Giver of golden days and golden song;
Nor is it by an all-unhappy plan
You bear the name of me, his constant Magian.
Yet ah! from any other that it came,
Lest fated to my fate you be, as to my name.
When at first those tidings did they bring,
My heart turned troubled at the ominous thing:
Though well may such a title him endower,
For whom a poet's prayer implores a poet's power.
The Assisian, who kept plighted faith to three,
To Song, to Sanctitude, and Poverty,
(In two alone of whom most singers prove
A fatal faithfulness of during love!);
He the sweet Sales, of whom we scarcely ken
How God he could love more, he so loved men;
The crown and crowned of Laura and Italy;
And Fletcher's fellow—from these, and not from me,
Take you your name, and take your legacy!

Or, if a right successive you declare
When worms, or ivies, intertwine my hair,
Take but this Poesy that now followeth
My clayey hest with sullen servile breath,
Made then your happy freedman by testating death.
My song I do but hold for you in trust,
I ask you but to blossom from my dust.
When you have compassed all weak I began,
Diviner poet, and ah! diviner man;
The man at feud with the perduring child
In you before Song's altar nobly reconciled;

From the wise heavens I half shall smile to see
How little a world, which owned you, needed me.
If, while you keep the vigils of the night,
For your wild tears make darkness all too bright,
Some lone orb through your lonely window peeps,
As it played lover over your sweet sleeps;
Think it a golden crevice in the sky,
Which I have pierced but to behold you by.

And when, immortal mortal, droops your head,
And you, the child of deathless song, are dead;
Then, as you search with unaccustomed glance
The ranks of Paradise for my countenance,
Turn not your tread along the Uranian sod
Among the bearded counsellors of God;
For if in Eden as on Earth are we,
I sure shall keep a younger company:
Pass where beneath their rangèd gonfalons
The starry cohorts shake their shielded suns,
The dreadful mass of their enridgèd spears;
Pass where majestical the eternal peers,
The stately choice of the great Saintdom, meet—
A silvern segregation, globed complete
In sandalled shadow of the Triune feet;
Pass by where wait, young poet-wayfarer,
Your cousined clusters, emulous to share
With you the roseal lightnings burning 'mid their hair;
Pass the crystalline sea, the Lampads seven:—
Look for me in the nurseries of Heaven.

TO OLIVIA

I fear to love thee, Sweet, because
Love's the ambassador of loss;
White flake of childhood, clinging so
To my soiled raiment, thy shy snow
At tenderest touch will shrink and go.
Love me not, delightful child.
My heart, by many snares beguiled,
Has grown timorous and wild.
It would fear thee not at all,
Wert thou not so harmless-small.
Because thy arrows, not yet dire,
Are still unbarbed with destined fire,
I fear thee more than hadst thou stood
Full-panoplied in womanhood.

LITTLE JESUS

Ex ore infantium, Deus, et lactentium perfecisti laudem

Little Jesus, wast Thou shy
Once, and just so small as I?
And what did it feel like to be
Out of Heaven, and just like me?
Didst Thou sometimes think of *there,*
And ask where all the angels were?
I should think that I would cry
For my house all made of sky;
I would look about the air,
And wonder where my angels were;
And at waking 'twould distress me—
Not an angel there to dress me!

[71]

Hadst Thou ever any toys,
Like us little girls and boys?
And didst Thou play in Heaven with all
The angels that were not too tall,
With stars for marbles? Did the things
Play *Can you see me?* through their wings?
And did Thy Mother let Thee spoil
Thy robes, with playing on *our* soil?
How nice to have them always new
In Heaven, because 'twas quite clean blue!
Didst Thou kneel at night to pray,
And didst Thou join Thy hands, this way?
And did they tire sometimes, being young,
And make the prayer seem very long?
And dost Thou like it best, that we
Should join our hands to pray to Thee?
I used to think, before I knew,
The prayer not said unless we do.
And did Thy Mother at the night
Kiss Thee, and fold the clothes in right?
And didst Thou feel quite good in bed,
Kissed, and sweet, and Thy prayers said?

Thou canst not have forgotten all
That it feels like to be small:
And Thou know'st I cannot pray
To Thee in my father's way—
When Thou wast so little, say,
Couldst Thou talk Thy Father's way?—
So, a little Child, come down
And hear a child's tongue like Thy own;
Take me by the hand and walk,

And listen to my baby-talk.
To Thy Father show my prayer
(He will look, Thou art so fair),
And say: "O Father, I, Thy Son,
Bring the prayer of a little one."

And He will smile, that children's tongue
Has not changed since Thou wast young!

DREAM-TRYST

The breaths of kissing night and day
Were mingled in the eastern Heaven:
    Throbbing with unheard melody
Shook Lyra all its star-chord seven:
      When the dusk shrunk cold, and light trod shy,
        And dawn's grey eyes were troubled grey;
      And souls went palely up the sky,
        And mine to Lucidé.

There was no change in her sweet eyes
    Since last I saw those sweet eyes shine;
There was no change in her deep heart
    Since last that deep heart knocked at mine.
      Her eyes were clear, her eyes were Hope's,
        Wherein did ever come and go
      The sparkle of the fountain-drops
        From her sweet soul below.

The chambers in the house of dreams
    Are fed with so divine an air,
That Time's hoar wings grow young therein,
    And they who walk there are most fair.
      I joyed for me, I joyed for her,
        Who with the Past meet girt about:
      Where our last kiss still warms the air,
        Nor can her eyes go out.

[74]

AN ARAB LOVE-SONG

The hunched camels of the night*
Trouble the bright
And silver waters of the moon.
The Maiden of the Morn will soon
Through Heaven stray and sing,
Star gathering.

Now while the dark about our loves is strewn,
Light of my dark, blood of my heart, O come!
And night will catch her breath up, and be dumb.

Leave thy father, leave thy mother
And thy brother;
Leave the black tents of thy tribe apart!
Am I not thy father and thy brother,
And thy mother?
And thou—what needest with thy tribe's black tents
Who hast the red pavilion of my heart?

LOVE AND THE CHILD

'Why do you so clasp me,
    And draw me to your knee?
Forsooth, you do but chafe me,
    I pray you let me be:
I will be loved but now and then
    When it liketh me!'

* Cloud-shapes observed by travellers in the East.

So I heard a young child,
   A thwart child, a young child
Rebellious against love's arms,
   Make its peevish cry.

To the tender God I turn:—
   'Pardon, Love most High!
For I think those arms were even Thine,
   And that child was even I.'

A DEAD ASTRONOMER

Stephen Perry, S. J.

Starry amorist, starward gone,
Thou art—what thou didst gaze upon!
Passed through thy golden garden's bars,
Thou seest the Gardener of the Stars.

She, about whose moonèd brows
Seven stars make seven glows,
Seven light for seven woes;
She, like thine own Galaxy,
All lustres in one purity:—
What said'st thou, Astronomer,
When thou did'st discover *her?*
When thy hand its tube let fall,
Thou found'st the fairest Star of all!

NOCTURN

I walk, I only,
Not I only wake;
Nothing is, this sweet night,
But doth couch and wake
For its love's sake;
Everything, this sweet night,
Couches with its mate.
For whom but for the stealthy-visitant sun
Is the naked moon
Tremulous and elate?
The heaven hath the earth
Its own and all apart;
The hushèd pool holdeth
A star to its heart.
You may think the rose sleepeth,
But though she folded is,
The wind doubts her sleeping;
Not all the rose sleeps,
But smiles in her sweet heart
For crafty bliss.
The wind lieth with the rose,
And when he stirs, she stirs in her repose;
The wind hath the rose,
And the rose her kiss.
Ah, mouth of me!
Is it then that this
Seemeth much to thee?—
I wander only.
The rose hath her kiss.

THE KINGDOM OF GOD

'In no Strange Land'

O world invisible, we view thee,
O world intangible, we touch thee,
O world unknowable, we know thee,
Inapprehensible, we clutch thee!

Does the fish soar to find the ocean,
The eagle plunge to find the air—
That we ask of the stars in motion
If they have rumour of thee there?

Not where the wheeling systems darken,
And our benumbed conceiving soars!—
The drift of pinions, would we hearken,
Beats at our own clay-shuttered doors.

The angels keep their ancient places;—
Turn but a stone, and start a wing!
'Tis ye, 'tis your estrangèd faces,
That miss the many-splendoured thing.

But (when so sad thou canst not sadder)
Cry;—and upon thy so sore loss
Shall shine the traffic of Jacob's ladder
Pitched betwixt Heaven and Charing Cross.

Yea, in the night, my Soul, my daughter,
Cry,—clinging Heaven by the hems;
And lo, Christ walking on the water
Not of Gennesareth, but Thames!

TO W. M.

O Tree of many branches! One thou hast
Thou barest not, but graftedst on thee. Now,
Should all men's thunders break on thee, and leave
Thee reft of bough and blossom, that one branch
Shall cling to thee, my Father, Brother, Friend,
Shall cling to thee, until the end of end.

ENVOY

Go, songs, for ended is our brief, sweet play;
   Go, children of swift joy and tardy sorrow:
And some are sung, and that was yesterday,
   And some unsung, and that may be to-morrow.

Go forth; and if it be o'er stony way,
   Old joy can lend what newer grief must borrow:
And it was sweet, and that was yesterday,
   And sweet is sweet, though purchasèd with sorrow.

Go, songs, and come not back from your far way:
   And if men ask you why ye smile and sorrow,
Tell them ye grieve, for your hearts know To-day,
   Tell them ye smile, for your eyes know To-morrow.

(IPL)--International Pocket Library
THEATER:

COUNTESS JULIE. August Strindberg. See **THREE PLAYS**.

DREAMY KID. Eugene O'Neill. See **FIVE MODERN PLAYS**.

FAREWELL SUPPER. Arthur Schnitzler. See **FIVE MODERN PLAYS**.

FATHER (THE). August Strindberg. 1434-9 $5.95

FIVE MODERN PLAYS: *Dreamy Kid, Farewell Supper, Sisters Tragedy, Lost Silk Hat, Intruder*. 1435-7 $5.95

IMPORTANCE OF BEING EARNEST. Oscar Wilde. 1442-x $5.95

INTRUDER. Maurice Maeterlinck. See **FIVE MODERN PLAYS**.

IRISH PLAYS--THREE. *Land of Heart's Desire, Twisting of the Rope, Riders to the Sea*. 1457-8 $5.95

LAND OF HEART'S DESIRE. W. B. Yeats. See **IRISH PLAYS (THREE)**.

LOST SILK HAT. Edward Dunsany. See **FIVE MODERN PLAYS**.

LOWER DEPTHS. Maxim Gorki. From Russian by Hopkins. 1445-4 $5.95

OUTLAW. August Strindberg. See **THREE PLAYS**.

RIDERS TO THE SEA. John M. Synge. See **IRISH PLAYS (THREE)**.

ROMEO AND JULIET. Shakespeare, Bandello, DaPorto, Masuccio. 0-9378-3232-4 $19.95

SALOMÉ. Oscar Wilde, Ill. by Aubrey Beardsley. 1467-5 $5.95

SEA GULL and TRAGEDIAN IN SPITE OF HIMSELF. Anton Chekhov. Trans. by O. F. Murphy. 1454-3 $5.95

SECOND SHEPHERD PLAY. Lisl Beer. 1246-x $3.95

SISTERS TRAGEDY. Richard Hughes. See **FIVE MODERN PLAYS**.

STRONGER. Auguste Strindberg. See **THREE PLAYS**.

THREE PLAYS. *Countess Julie, Stronger, Outlaw*. A. Strindberg. Trans. by and with notes by E. & W. Oland. 1458-6 $5.95

TWISTING OF THE ROPE. Douglas Hyde. See **IRISH PLAYS (THREE)**.

LITERATURE--HISTORY:

ARMOURY LIGHT VERSE. Richard Armour. 1424-1 $5.95

BRAZILIAN TALES. *Attendant's Confession, Fortune Teller, Aunt Zeze Tears, Pigeons*. 1426-8 $5.95

CANTERVILLE GHOST. Oscar Wilde. 1429-2 $5.95

CARGOES--BEST SEA STORIES. W.W. Jacobs. 1430-6 $5.95

CECCO, THE WAY I AM AND WAS. Angiolieri, bilingual 2000-4 $12.95

CIVIL DISOBEDIENCE. H. D. Thoreau. See **MODERN ESSAYS**.

COLOURED STARS--50 ASIATIC LOVE SONGS. E. Mathers. 1432-2 $5.95

DANTE IN THE 20TH CENTURY. Borges et al. 0-9378-3216-2 $25.95

FULL MOON IS RISING. Basho, haikus. 1651-1 $15.95 c.